THE STORY OF
THE WHITE HOUSE

by Kate Waters

SCHOLASTIC INC.

New York   Toronto   London   Auckland   Sydney

I Pray Heaven to Bestow
The Best of Blessings on
THIS HOUSE and on ALL that shall hereafter
Inhabit it. May none but Honest
And Wise Men ever rule under This Roof.

— *John Adams to his wife,*
Abigail, in a letter written
the day after he moved
into the White House.

The White House belongs to
everyone in our country.
The president of the United States
works and lives there.

U.S.A.

Washington,
D.C.

*Alaska   *Hawaii

The White House is in Washington, D.C., the capital
of our country.
The people who run our country work there.
The city is filled with important buildings.

*Alaska and Hawaii are out of scale and out of position.

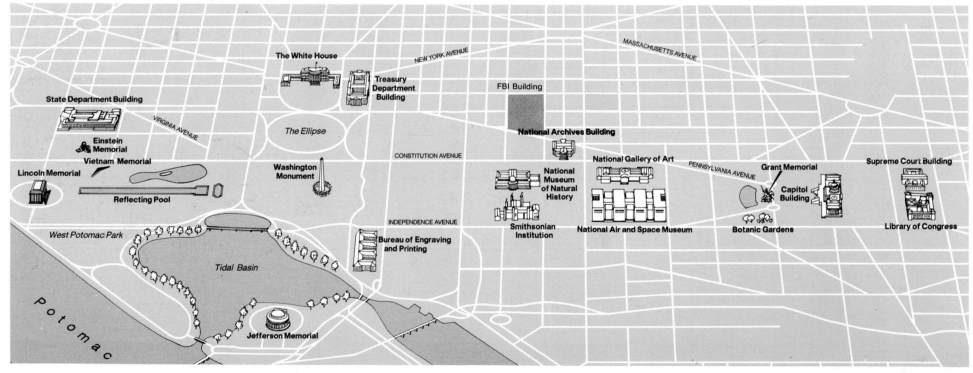

The White House

Treasury
Department
Building

FBI Building

State Department Building

NEW YORK AVENUE

MASSACHUSETTS AVENUE

VIRGINIA AVENUE

The Ellipse

National Archives Building

Einstein
Memorial

CONSTITUTION AVENUE

National Gallery of Art

PENNSYLVANIA AVENUE

Grant Memorial

Supreme Court Building

Vietnam Memorial

Lincoln Memorial

Washington
Monument

National
Museum
of Natural
History

Capitol
Building

Reflecting Pool

INDEPENDENCE AVENUE

Smithsonian
Institution

National Air and Space Museum

Botanic Gardens

Library of Congress

West Potomac Park

Bureau of Engraving
and Printing

Tidal Basin

P o t o m a c

Jefferson Memorial

The Reading Room in the Library of Congress

The Justice Department

New paper money

The Library of Congress has one copy of every single book copyrighted in the United States. It is the largest library in the world.

New money for the whole country is printed at the Bureau of Engraving and Printing.

The Congress meets in the Capitol Building.

Government lawyers work in the Justice Department.

In the Supreme Court Building, nine Supreme Court justices decide whether rulings made in other courts are good or bad.

The Capitol Building

The Supreme Court

View into the Red Room

Important decisions are made in the
White House.
Leaders from all around the world
come to meet with the president.
The house is a symbol of our
country, and of our kind of
government, which is called a
democracy.
Like most big old houses, there are
stories told about the people who
lived there and the special things
that happened there.
Here is the story of the White House.

Washington, D.C., seen from across the Potomac River. (George Cooke, 1833)

Washington, D.C., has not always looked like it does today.
Once it was a sleepy little village with only a few buildings.
There were no good roads into the village, and no good docks for boats.

About two hundred years ago, when the United States was a brand-new country, people began to talk about where the president should live.
Should the president live in the North or the South?
Should the president's house be a palace, like kings live in, or a simpler house?

The Franklin Square house, New York City

The Macomb house on Broadway, New York City

The Morris house, Philadelphia

While Congress debated what to build and where to build it, our first president, George Washington, lived in three houses.

The first two were in New York City.

The third was in Philadelphia, Pennsylvania.

Finally, Washington decided to compromise.

He picked a patch of land on the Potomac River.

Both Maryland and Virginia gave land for the new capital.

The land was on the border of the North and the South. (At this time, there were no Western states!)

George Washington named the land the District of Columbia, in honor of Christopher Columbus.

Benjamin Banneker

President Washington hired people
    to plan a new city.
Washington, D.C., is one of the
    only cities in the world that
    was designed before it was
    built.
First, Benjamin Banneker and
    Andrew Ellicott made maps of
    the land.

Andrew Ellicott

Pierre Charles L'Enfant

Then, Pierre Charles L'Enfant decided where to put the roads.

Washington decided to put the Capitol Building on a hill at one end of the city, and the president's house on a hill at the other end.

Now it was time to decide what kind of house to build for the president.

Pierre Charles L'Enfant's city plan

Thomas Jefferson suggested having a contest.
He advertised the contest in newspapers across the country.

A committee picked a simple but elegant design by James Hoban, a young Irish American architect.

The first stone was laid on October 13, 1792.

It took eight years to finish enough of the house to make it livable.

Even then, Washington, D.C., was a rough, unfinished city.

The Capitol Building wasn't completed yet, and congressmen lived in boardinghouses surrounded by farmland.

John Adams, the second president of the United States, moved into a cold, damp White House in November 1800.

Abigail Adams hung her laundry up to dry in the East Room. She thought it would be bad manners to hang the president's laundry outside.

James Hoban

James Hoban's winning drawing

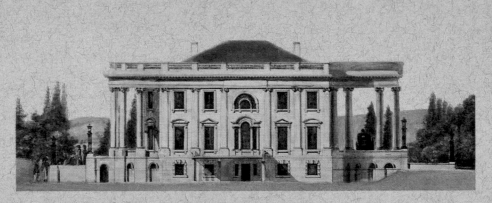

Proposed additions to the White House.

By the time our third president, Thomas Jefferson, moved into the White House in 1801, most of the outside structures were finished.

The White House was the largest residential house in America!

Jefferson ordered wallpaper and furniture from France.

Every president since has ordered special things for the house.

Today, you can see chairs that people sat on more than one hundred years ago!

During this time, the building was called The President's Palace, and then The President's House.

Gilbert Stuart's portrait of George Washington

Then James Madison was elected president.
During his term of office, the United States went to
war with England.
It was the War of 1812.
As the British troops got close to Washington,
Madison's wife, Dolley, ordered a carriage to pick
her up and take her to safety.
But she would not leave the house until two men
agreed to take down the famous portrait of
George Washington.
The troops set fire to the Capitol Building and the
White House.
Today, the picture that Dolley saved is the only thing
that has been in the White House since it first
opened.

The burning of Washington, D.C., by the British in 1812, with
the White House in the background. (Wash drawing)

After the fire

About 1831

When the war was over, the house was rebuilt
and repainted white to cover the smoke marks.
People began to call it the White House.

1860

About 1900

People all over the world think of the White House as the symbol of our country.

The White House stands for freedom.

The president signs laws that affect all of us.

Leaders from other countries come to the White House to meet with the president.

There are also parties and special ceremonies at the White House.

You can visit the White House, too.
It is open for tours almost every day of the year.
More than one million people visit every year!

Some lucky visitors even see the president or the first lady walking down the halls.
People who visit see only part of this big house.

There are 132 rooms in all.
On the official tour, visitors only see seven rooms and three halls.
Each room is filled with precious old furniture and objects.
The White House is also a museum.

When you enter the White House, the first thing you see is the Secret Service station.
Secret Service people are specially trained police officers.
You may notice the little earphones in their ears.
They can give and receive messages about any possible danger.

The State Dining Room

These are some of the rooms you can see on the official White House
    tour.
The State Dining Room is big enough for 140 people to sit down to eat!
The East Room is the biggest room in the White House.
This is where the president and first lady give parties.
Sometimes workers set up a stage for music concerts and dance
    performances.
Presidents have also held press conferences here.

The East Room

The Entrance Hall

The White House library has 2,700 books in it.
All of the books are by American authors.
The president's family can take books from here to read.

The Library

The other famous rooms you can see have color names.

The Green Room

The Blue Room

The Red Room

Let's look at some of the rooms most people never see.

The president's office is in the West Wing of the White House.

The West Wing

It is called the Oval Office because it is shaped like this:

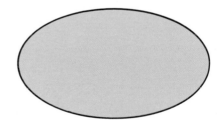

There are two flags behind the president's desk.
One is the flag of our country.
The other is the Presidential Flag.
Each president chooses his own furnishings.

The Oval Office

There are two kitchens and one pantry in the White House.

White House chefs sometimes have to make food for more than one hundred people a day!

The Lincoln Bedroom

The Queen's Bedroom

There are eleven bedrooms and thirty-two
    bathrooms!
But only the president and the first lady and their
    guests sleep there.
There are two famous bedrooms in the private part
    of the White House.

Once, a president's dog had
    puppies in a White House
    bedroom!

An Autopen

All together, ninety-six people work in the residential part of the White House.

In the Office of Correspondence, people read the letters that the president gets.

Almost 15,000 letters are delivered to the White House every day.

Every letter is answered with at least a card. That does not mean the president signs each one.

There is a machine, called an Autopen, that signs the president's name!

Newspaper and television reporters from around the country have offices in the West Wing.

They are ready whenever the president decides to hold a press conference.

Telephone operators answer almost 50,000 calls every day. Most of the calls are for the president.
Today the telephone operators use computers, but not long ago all the calls were connected by hand!

The White House switchboard in 1955

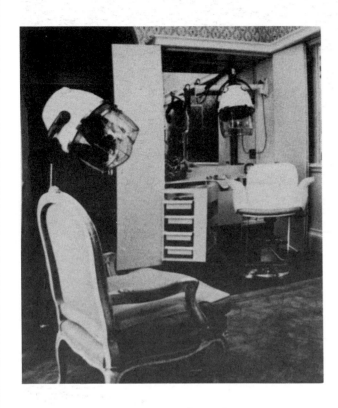

The president and his family have
    to be careful where they go
    outside the White House.
They have to have Secret Service
    guards all the time.
So, long ago, presidents decided
    that it would be easier to have
    some services available inside
    the White House.

At different times there has been a barbershop, a
    beauty salon, and a clinic.
For quiet family fun and exercise, there is a bowling
    alley, a movie theater, a small gym, and a game
    room.

Outside on the lawn, there is a swimming pool
surrounded by trees!

The lawns and gardens outside the White House fence are called the President's Park.

The park is beautiful in every season.

Every year, no matter who is president, there is a
special party for young people at the White
House.
On the Monday after Easter, there is an Easter egg
roll.

At Christmastime, visitors can see the huge National
Christmas tree.
It is in the park across the street from the White
House.

The White House has grown and
    changed as our country has
    grown and changed.
Each family who has lived there has
    left its mark.
And every American can dream and
    plan to grow up and live there.

Fun Facts to Know About the White House Residents

1. **George Washington** is said to have donated some of his own silver spoons and forks when our new country needed silver and gold to make money.

2. **John Adams** is said to have held the first fireworks display at the White House.

3. **Thomas Jefferson** had a pet mockingbird that flew freely around the White House unless Jefferson had guests.

4. **James Madison's** wife, Dolley, loved to give parties. She regularly served ice cream to her guests.

5. **James Monroe** toured the whole country while he was president. At that time St. Louis was the most western city in our country!

6. **John Quincy Adams** was the first president to be photographed.

7. **Andrew Jackson's** supporters came to a party at the White House after he was elected. They broke dishes and stood on the furniture in their muddy boots.

8. **Martin Van Buren** was a widower. He lived in the White House with his four sons.

9. **William Henry Harrison** was president only thirty-two days. He caught pneumonia and died after standing outside for hours during his inauguration.

10. **John Tyler** was the first president to get married while in office.

11. **James K. Polk's** wife was very strict. She did not allow card playing or dancing or drinking in the White House.

12. **Zachary Taylor** brought his horse, Old Whitey, with him to the White House. Old Whitey used to stand on the White House lawn, eating the grass.

13. **Millard Fillmore** established the White House library. Before this time there was no permanent collection of books in the White House.

14. **Franklin Pierce** ordered the first bathtub for the White House. Many people were upset. They thought taking baths was not healthy and would make you sick!

15. **James Buchanan** was the only president who never married.

16. **Abraham Lincoln** used to walk alone at night to the War Department to find out news about the Civil War.

17. **Andrew Johnson** did not learn to read until he was seventeen years old. His parents had been too poor to send him to school.

18. **Ulysses S. Grant** helped set up Yellowstone National Park, which was our country's first national park.

19. **Rutherford B. Hayes** had the first telephone installed in the White House. Alexander Graham Bell, the inventor of the telephone, gave Hayes personal instructions on how to use it.

20. **James A. Garfied** could write with both hands. Sometimes he amused people by writing Greek with one hand and Latin with the other!

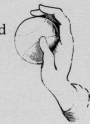

21. **Chester A. Arthur** thought the White House was too gloomy so he redecorated it. Twenty-four wagonloads of old furniture were carted away to make room for new, more fashionable furniture.

22 & 24. **Grover Cleveland** was both the twenty-second and twenty-fourth president. He is also the only president to have had his wedding inside the White House.

23. **Benjamin Harrison** had the White House wired for electricity, but he was afraid of getting shocked so he would not touch the switches!

25. **William McKinley's** picture is on the five-hundred-dollar bill. Guam, Hawaii, and Puerto Rico all became part of the United States during his term of office.

26. **Theodore Roosevelt** had the West Wing built onto the White House. He moved his office there so he could work in peace and quiet.

27. **William Howard Taft** started the tradition of the president throwing out the first ball at the beginning of the baseball season.

28. **Woodrow Wilson** was president when World War I began. He tried to keep our country out of the war. Then, when we had to go to war, Wilson said he hoped it would be the "war to end all wars."

29. **Warren G. Harding** was the first president to give a speech over the radio.

30. **Calvin Coolidge** liked to sit outside at night to think and relax. But so many people stopped and pointed at him that he finally gave up and sat inside.

31. **Herbert C. Hoover** was the first president to be born west of the Mississippi River.

32. **Franklin D. Roosevelt** got permission to build a swimming pool and add a movie theater in the White House.

33. **Harry S. Truman** and his wife, Bess, lived across the street from the White House in Blair House while the White House had some much-needed construction work done.

34. **Dwight D. Eisenhower** was the first president to use a helicopter that took off and landed on the White House lawn.

35. **John F. Kennedy's** young son, John, Jr., used to hide under the president's desk. John, Jr., called the desk "my house."

36. **Lyndon B. Johnson** was the first president to fly all the way around the world visiting other governments.

37. **Richard Milhous Nixon** was the first president to resign from office.

38. **Gerald R. Ford** swam laps in the White House pool almost every day. Once he gave a press conference while he was swimming!

39. **"Jimmy" Carter's** daughter Amy had a tree house on the South Grounds of the White House. Sometimes she watched special ceremonies from there.

40. **Ronald Reagan** was the first movie actor to be elected president.

41. **George Bush** invites tennis champions to play with him on the White House tennis courts.

White House Portraits

1. George Washington (1789 - 1797) Martha Dandridge (Custis) Washington

2. John Adams (1797 - 1801) Abigail Smith Adams

3. Thomas Jefferson (1801 - 1809) *†Martha Wayles (Skelton) Jefferson *Martha Jefferson Randolph *†Maria "Polly" Wayles Jefferson Eppes

4. James Madison (1809 - 1817) Dorothea"Dolley" Payne (Todd) Madison

5. James Monroe (1817 - 1825) Elizabeth Kortright Monroe *Eliza Monroe Hay

6. John Quincy Adams (1825 - 1829) Louisa Catherine Johnson Adams

7. Andrew Jackson (1829 - 1837) Rachel Donelson (Robards) Jackson *Emily Tennessee Donelson *Sarah Yorke Jackson

8. Martin Van Buren (1837 - 1841) Hannah Hoes Van Buren *Angelica Singleton Van Buren

9. William Henry Harrison (1841 - 1841) Anna Tuthill Symmes Harrison *†Jane Irwin Harrison *Jane Irwin Findlay

10. John Henry Tyler (1841 - 1845) Letitia Christian Tyler *Priscilla Cooper Tyler *Letitia Tyler Semple

Julia Gardiner Tyler

11. James K. Polk (1845 - 1849) Sarah Childress Polk

12. Zachary Taylor (1849 - 1850) *†Magaret Mackall Smith Taylor *Mary Elizabeth "Betty" Taylor Bliss

13. Millard Fillmore (1850 - 1853) Abigail Powers Fillmore *Mary Abigail Fillmore Caroline Carmichael (McIntosh) Fillmore

14. Franklin Pierce (1853 - 1857) Jane Means Appleton Pierce *†Abby Kent Means

15. James Buchanan (1857 - 1861) *Harriet Lane

16. Abraham Lincoln (1861 - 1865) Mary Todd Lincoln

17. Andrew Johnson (1865 - 1869) Eliza McCardle Johnson *Martha Johnson Patterson

18. Ulysses S. Grant (1869 - 1877) Julia Dent Grant

19. Rutherford B. Hayes (1877 - 1881) Lucy Ware Webb Hayes

20. James A. Garfield (1881 - 1881) Lucretia Rudolph Garfield

21. Chester A. Arthur (1881 - 1885) Ellen Lewis Herndon Arthur *Mary Arthur McElroy

22 & 24. Grover Cleveland (1885 - 1889) (1893 - 1897) *Rose Elizabeth Cleveland Frances Folsom Cleveland

23. Benjamin Harrison (1889 - 1893) Caroline Lavinia Scott Harrison *Mary Scott Harrison McKee Mary Scott Lord (Dimmick) Harrison

25. William McKinley (1897 - 1901) Ida Saxton McKinley

26. Theodore Roosevelt (1901 - 1909) Alice Hathaway Lee Roosevelt Edith Kermit Carow Roosevelt

27. William Howard Taft (1909 - 1913) Helen Herron Taft *Helen Herron Taft

28. Woodrow Wilson (1913 - 1921) Ellen Louise Axson Wilson *Helen Woodrow Bones *Margaret Woodrow Wilson

Edith Bolling (Galt) Wilson

29. Warren G. Harding (1921 - 1923) Florence Kling (De Wolfe) Harding

30. Calvin Coolidge
(1923 - 1929)

Grace Anna
Goodhue
Coolidge

31. Herbert C.
Hoover
(1929 - 1933)

Lou Henry
Hoover

32. Franklin D.
Roosevelt
(1933 - 1945)

Anna Eleanor
Roosevelt
Roosevelt

33. Harry S. Truman
(1945 - 1953)

Elizabeth "Bess"
Virginia Wallace
Truman

34. Dwight D.
Eisenhower
(1953 - 1961)

Mary "Mamie"
Geneva Doud
Eisenhower

35. John F. Kennedy
(1961 - 1963)

Jacqueline
"Jackie"
Lee Bouvier
Kennedy

36. Lyndon B.
Johnson
(1963 - 1969)

Claudia "Lady
Bird" Alta
Taylor Johnson

37. Richard
Milhouse Nixon
(1969 - 1974)

Thelma Catherine
Patricia "Pat"
Ryan Nixon

38. Gerald R. Ford
(1974 - 1977)

Elizabeth "Betty"
Warren Bloomer
Ford

39. "Jimmy" James
E. Carter
(1977 - 1981)

Rosalynn Smith
Carter

40. Ronald Reagan
(1981 - 1989)

Anne Frances
"Nancy" Robbins
(Davis) Reagan

41. George Bush
(1989 -   )

Barbara Pierce
Bush

*These women were not the president's wives. They were relatives
who served as official White House hostesses when the president
was a widower, or the first lady died during the president's term
of office or became too ill to entertain. James Buchanan was the
only president who never married.

†Portrait unavailable

A Selected Bibliography for Children:

Blassingame, Wyatt. *The Look-It-Up Book of the Presidents*. New York: Random House, 1990.

Cary, Sturges F. *Arrow Book of Presidents*. New York: Scholastic Inc., 1980.

Fisher, Leonard Everett. *The White House*. New York: Holiday House, 1989.

Krementz, Jill. *A Visit to Washington, D.C.* New York: Scholastic Hardcover, 1987.

Kutner, Nanette. *The White House Saga*. New York: Atheneum, 1962.

Miller, Natalie. *The Story of the White House*. Chicago: Children's Press, 1966.

Munro, Roxie. *The Inside-Outside Book of Washington, D.C.* New York: E.P. Dutton, 1987.

Provensen, Alice. *The Buck Stops Here*. New York: Harper & Row, Publishers, 1990.

Smith, Irene. *Washington, D.C.* Chicago: Rand McNally & Company, 1964.

Sullivan, George. *How the White House Really Works*. New York: E.P. Dutton, 1989.

Turck, Mary. *Washington, D.C.* New York: Crestwood House, 1989.

A Selected Bibliography for Adults (although children will love the photographs and illustrations):

Aikman, Lonnelle. *The Living White House*. Washington, D.C.: The White House Historical Association, 1987.

Bruse, Preston, et al. *From the Door of the White House*. New York: Lothrop, 1984.

Ryan, William, and Desmond Guinness. *The White House: An Architectural History*. New York: McGraw-Hill Book Company, 1980.

White House Historical Association. *The White House: An Historical Guide*. Washington, D.C.: White House Historical Association, 1979.

Index

(Page numbers in *italics* indicate illustrations of the subjects listed.)

Photo Credits

AP/Wide World Photos: p. 19 (bottom); p. 22; p. 25; p. 26 (both); p. 27 (left), p. 38 (#41 right).

The Bettmann Archive: p. 7; p. 13; p. 14 (bottom right).

Bill Fitz-Patrick/The White House: p. 21 (close-up of seal).

Cynthia Breeden/The White House: p. 24.

Culver Pictures: p. 11 (top).

Gamma-Liaison: p. 23 (bottom); p. 30.

The Granger Collection: p. 8 (all); p. 9 (right); p. 10 (top left); p. 12 (top); back jacket.

International Autopen Co.: p. 24 (left).

Leo de Wys, Inc.: pp. 2–3 by Everett Johnson; p. 15 by Alon Reininger; p. 16 by J. Messerschmidt.

The Library of Congress: p. 1, 36, 37, 38.

The Schomberg Collection: p. 9 (top left).

The White House Historical Association: p. 6; p. 10 (map); p. 11 (bottom); p. 13 (right); p. 14 (top left, top right, bottom left); p. 17; p. 18 (left and right); p. 19 (top); p. 20 (left, middle, right); p. 21 (top and bottom right); p. 23 (top left and right); p. 28 (left); pp. 32–33; p. 38 (#41 left); p. 38 (#37 right); p. 38 (#40 left and right).

Wide World Photos, Inc.: p. 5 (all but top center); p. 28 (right); p. 29 (top and bottom); p. 31 (right); p. 38 (#38 right); p. 38 (#38 left).

UPI/Bettmann Newsphotos: p. 27 (right); p. 38 (#37 left).

U.S. Bureau of Printing and Engraving: p. 5 (top center); p. 38 (left and right).

To my parents with love.

Acknowledgments

Many thanks are due to Mr. Rex Scouten, Curator of the White House, and his staff, not only for vetting this book but also for enthusiastically answering questions of the most minute sort; to the Secret Service staff in the White House for answering my many questions and for letting me linger and listen to questions children ask; to the research staffs of the Library of Congress and the New York Public Library; to Lucy Evankow, Chief Librarian of Scholastic Inc.; to Don Stoll for recommending the Hotel Washington, which became my home-away-from-home; to Dianne Hess, my editor; to Nancy Hanes, for last-minute research assistance; and most particularly, to Deborah Thompson, whose innovative and exhaustive photo research gave us a glorious selection of photographs, drawings, and engravings with which to tell this story.

ISBN 0-590-43334-2

12 11 10 9 8 7 6 5 4 3 2 1   2 3 4 5 6 7/9

Printed in the U.S.A.   09

Map on page 4 by Paul Pugliese   Book design by Laurie McBarnette